Angels
in the
Pigpen

❧⚜❧

DAVID TESTER

Copyright © 2014 David Tester
All rights reserved.

ISBN: 1500570192
ISBN 13: 9781500570194
Library of Congress Control Number: 2014913042
CreateSpace Independent Publishing Platform
North Charleston, South Carolina

Pig Kisses!

A Story of God,

His Angels,

and Wilbur

To Madison and Natalie:

Wilbur would have loved you very much.

Once upon a time there was a city preacher and a pig.

This is a true story of their meeting and lifelong friendship.

Contents

Appreciation viii
Chapter 1 A Flat Pig 1
Chapter 2 Going to Market 6
Chapter 3 Growing Pains, Mudholes, and Potty Habits 9
Chapter 4 Sometimes You Can't Use the Bathroom 13
Chapter 5 Pigs May Not Be What We Think They Are 16
Chapter 6 The Factory and the UPS Man 19
Chapter 7 Sometimes You Miss the Obvious or Pigs Can Plow 21
Chapter 8 Relaxing Time 23
Chapter 9 The Wash Job 26
Chapter 10 Who's That Knocking? 29
Chapter 11 I Smell Bacon Frying 31
Chapter 12 Town without Pity 34
Chapter 13 Moving Time 38
Chapter 14 Settling In 42
Chapter 15 Yoo-hoo and Moon Pies 44
Chapter 16 And You Thought You Didn't like Going to the Dentist? .. 46
Chapter 17 A Pig Girdle? 50
Chapter 18 Running Water and the Pig Fountain 54
Chapter 19 Calling All Cars 56
Chapter 20 Cheez Doodles and the Big Mean Dog 59
Chapter 21 Get in the Trailer, Wilbur! 61
Chapter 22 We Don't Have a Record for Oldest Pig 65
Chapter 23 Angels in the Pigpen 67
Chapter 24 Will Animals Be in Heaven? 71
Epilogue 75

Appreciation

Tommy Quarles, Gentlemen Farmer.

Dr. Ernest Stuart, Veterinarian extraordinaire.

Leland Lumley, Gentlemen Farmer;
Vice President, Greenwood Equipment.

Jerry Duncan, Gentlemen Farmer.

Coronaca Baptist Church, for loving Wilbur and giving him a wonderful place to live.

CHAPTER 1

A Flat Pig

B lood flowed from where his tail should have been. Barely four pounds, the tiny pig lay helpless, unable to stand. He looked like roadkill. This city preacher didn't know anything about pigs. Yet staring into his face, I knew this one was not long for the world.

It was a frigid December night when our son, David, arrived home with this tiny newborn creature. David carefully caressed the animal as though he were carrying precious cargo. "He was over at Tommy's farm," David said, avoiding my eyes but staring at this tiny, dying swine. "I found him stuck in the feed bin, and the other pigs had eaten his tail off."

Finally David looked me square in the face, his eyes pleading for compassion for this infant pig.

"He's really sick." David's speech stumbled. "Can we keep him?"

David was our teenage son. Tall and thin with dark eyes and hair, he looked shockingly like a much younger me. But tonight, as he was holding the bleeding, dying pig, I could see only the compassion of his mother radiating from his pleading eyes.

"You must be kidding," I replied, hoping that a quick, terse reply would squelch his plaintive empathy, which was gently and rapidly invading my heart. "David, we don't know anything about pigs. And what if he got better, what would we do with him?"

"I dunno," David admitted, but the concern for the feeble pig did not leave his face.

Because I assumed the tiny piglet wouldn't survive the night, it seemed reasonable that we might as well make him comfortable. Retrieving a cardboard box and a towel, I told David, "Put him in the outside utility room, and we'll check on him in the morning."

The sun was peeking through the darkness as I crept out of bed and cracked the door to see if the piglet was still with us. I confess I had more feeling for the helpless creature than I allowed anyone to imagine. Anxiously I opened the utility door, and there he was: flat as a flapjack, yet still alive. I breathed a deep sigh and smiled. I had hoped he would make it.

Feeling sorry for the tiny being, I eased him into my arms and was delighted to detect a shallow breath. Running back inside, I yelled, "Get up! He's alive!"

Our daughter, Leslie, was home from college. Her heart is as beautiful as her image in the mirror. Leslie leapt into action. She scrambled through the closet to find a doll baby blanket that had been packed away long ago. Sitting in the rocker, she wrapped the piglet tightly, snuggling him close.

The questions flew. "What do we name him? What do we feed him?"

"I don't know. We've not had a pig in our home before."

"Let's call the vet."

"Oh sure," I said. My thoughts raced. *I can hear it already. See, Doc, we've got this flat pig and....*

However, we called. After listening to our explanation, the doctor laughed harder than I thought possible.

Following the vet's instructions, we found the doll baby bottle that matched the blanket, put orange Gatorade inside, and coaxed the nipple into the piglet's mouth. We did a lot of coaxing all day. As the sun set and shadows draped our home, we had no more than four exhausted people and a pig with an orange mouth to show for our efforts.

"I think this pig has pneumonia. We better take him to the vet."

"The vet?"

"You're going to make an appointment for a pig?"

"I bet they won't take him."

Finally I called. "Hello, Dr. Smith. Remember the pig we called about? Do you treat pigs?"

"They usually don't live long enough for me to see them. What seems to be wrong?"

"Pneumonia, I think. And he's flat. No bacon anywhere. He can't stand, just falls on his side."

"Well, bring him in and let's see. Boy, this will be a first. Never treated a pig."

The veterinarian's exam took only a few minutes. "You're right," the doctor said, pulling his glasses from his face as he turned toward our small family. "Pneumonia in both lungs. I'll give him a shot and send two needles home with you."

"You mean...?"

"You can give him a shot, can't you?"

"Oh yes. I give pigs shots quite often," I said, my voice dripping sarcasm. "By the way, Doc, how do you give a pig a shot?"

The pig shots were easier than I expected. But then, the piglet was too weak to protest.

Slowly, in response to the love and care of a doting family of four, the pig got better.

"Better keep him inside," David instructed us. Knowing the piglet couldn't tolerate the December cold, I found a new box and made a home for him in the laundry room.

Of course he didn't stay in the box. Leslie had him out of the box, watching his awkward, wobbly movements as he walked.

"We better put a diaper on him," my wife, Margaret, said, being realistic as she wiped her hands with a dish towel.

"What?" I asked incredulously. "A pig in a diaper?"

"Well, we just put him in a blanket," Leslie reminded us. "Haven't you heard of a pig in the blanket?"

"Okay, point made," I conceded, wondering where we could purchase a pig diaper.

Once diapers were found and purchased, the pig was one odd sight. A flat pig in a diaper, nursing a doll baby bottle of orange Gatorade.

Once he started eating, our pig-novice family discovered another fact about the anatomy of pigs. Pigs need two diapers. God made their plumbing farther apart than that of human babies'. One diaper wouldn't cut it. I mean, a pig going "Wee, wee, wee all the way home" is much better than "Wee, wee, wee in the home."

Unfortunately the two diapers didn't work either. We rolled with laughter as the rear diaper slid down when Wilbur tried to walk.

Yes, I had agreed that he needed a name. "If he's going to stay for a while, we can't just say, 'Here, pig.' How 'bout Wilbur?" I suggested.

"You mean from the movie?"

"Yeah. If there's ever been a terrific pig, he's it."

"Hello, Wilbur, welcome," David said with a grin.

CHAPTER 2

Going to Market

I love to munch!

We decided the laundry room would be Wilbur's new home. Great promises were made by David to take him out for bathroom breaks: "I promise I'll clean up after and feed him."

If there is a true American story, it's that when kids bring home a stray pet, they will not follow through on the elimination promises. The job always falls to Dad.

Therefore, that's what Wilbur and I did. In and out, out and in. But you know what? The little guy was a heart stealer. It is hard to explain how a pig became an important part of my life. I couldn't help but love him. In fact, our entire family quickly grew to love this tiny creature.

The days slipped into weeks, and Wilbur grew. That's what pigs do best. In addition, they excel in eating and sleeping, digging holes, and oinking.

Wilbur was feeling much better, and it was time for him to go back to Tommy's farm. "David, will you take him?" I naively asked. Then it hit me. Back to Tommy's farm? Growing bigger. Bacon...pork chops... *the market*!

"Wait a minute!" I said quickly. "No, we can't do that. I'll build him a small pen in the backyard."

Could a city preacher really be saying that? True, we lived in a rural area, but pig raising? What if I got a call to a city church and we moved? Then what? It's not like putting the family dog in the car.

I looked at Wilbur, and he looked at me while letting out the faintest sound of a grunt. It was as if he were saying, "Can I please stay with you?"

That did it. No way was this pig going to market. Let me get some wire and build a pen—wait, did I speak too soon? How do you do that? I've bought a doghouse, but they don't sell pigpens at Walmart.

At the hardware store, chicken wire seemed to be just right for a little pig's home. I decided to call it "pig wire" so Wilbur wouldn't think he was living in a chicken coop.

After lots of work, the pig wire stood with the support of a few sticks. Inside, I placed a small box filled with hay.

"Wilbur," I told him, "this is your new home."

Now you're going to think I'm crazy, but that pig and I bonded. I couldn't wait to leave the church and feed him at lunchtime.

One day I got a big scare. I parked in the front and rushed back to see him. I went to the pen, and that's when I noticed: Wilbur wasn't there! My heart dropped into my socks. "Oh no," I said.

Suddenly the hay pile exploded with excited pig—Wilbur had buried himself under mounds of warm hay. I hugged him, thankful he was safe.

Suppertime was filled with more play. You know, the way you would play with your dog. He zoomed around that small pen squealing with delight.

God must tell baby pigs how to root 'cause that's something Wilbur tried right off. What a sight. Nose down in the grass, poised like a steam shovel, he slowly began to dig in and lift up. Trouble was he had no weight to help; he was still skinny. Well, sir, his pork butt lifted straight off the ground and into the air, and there he was, two front hooves and nose balancing him so he looked like he was high diving.

I started bringing him Little Debbie cakes.

"Hey, Wilbur, want some chocolate milk to wash that down?"

He did. That's when I discovered that pigs can drink from a bottle. I would hold the Yoo-hoo to his mouth, and down it went. Well, actually, more ran down the outside than the inside. He seemed to really like this. I guess that's why we call them pigs.

CHAPTER 3

Growing Pains, Mudholes, and Potty Habits

Hi, I'm Wilbur.

Wilbur was growing, and fast. I'd spoiled him with sugar cakes and chocolate milk. He started to look like someone put a soda straw in his mouth and blew.

The small pen he lived in was touching him on all sides. He needed a larger home.

Well, here we go again. His new house was built farther out in the yard from ideas gleaned by riding around looking at pigpens.

Now that's a wonderful way to spend your afternoon. Especially when you discover most pens are "throw-togethers" made from almost any discarded object: tires, pieces of cars, old doors, used refrigerators, any piece of wood (size doesn't matter), and wire.

Another discovery: no books on pigpen plans exist. What to do? Wilbur's house just had to look more special than a one-hundred-car pileup on the freeway. No junkyard for this special pig.

I planned the house and set about building it. I sank the corner frames into the ground and drove the nails deep into the boards and used cloth fabric for a door. It was a strong new home. You could huff and you could puff and not blow it down. The howling rain could not enter, and the cold of winter was held at bay by his cloth door. The house had a fence post at the four corners and tin for the roof and walls. A foot of hay made a special mattress for Wilbur.

A strong wire fence gave him much freedom to romp and run.

Oh my, what a wonderful house. I put his name on the front in big bold red letters, "WILBUR." Word went out all around that no finer pigpen had ever been constructed. It was suitable for the front cover of *Shack and Gardens* magazine.

The big move-in day came. I picked Wilbur up, and he squealed loudly. Pigs do that when picked up; I don't know why. "Shut up, Wilbur, somebody's going to think I'm abusing you."

But he didn't—that is, till I set him down in his very own big yard. Snorting and oinking loudly, he ran all over checking things out.

In the days to come I would find out something else about pigs and especially about Wilbur. By themselves they are very clean animals. No, I'm not kidding. People always say, "Dirty as a pig." But that didn't apply to Wilbur.

When it came time for Wilbur to use the bathroom, he went far away from his house, all the way to the corner of the fence. Each and every time, this is where Wilbur used the toilet. *Every time.* The rain would pour, the snow would blow, the wind would howl, and the hail would fall. Nothing kept him from going in the exact same spot. Never failed, and even when he grew very old, he kept his personal space clean.

Six months went by, and it was time to make the pen bigger. So I took the back wall of the fence, where he used the bathroom, and moved it much farther out.

Wow! Did he have a big pigpen! You know what? Wilbur had used the bathroom in the same spot for those six months; you remember, the place farthest from his house. Well, that day I saw something amazing: he used the bathroom the farthest from this house he could get, by the new fence corner. Man, talk about a clean pig. Sure did make it easier to clean his pen.

Another thing pigs don't do: they don't sweat. So they have to cool off someway. That's why mudholes are their favorite places. Pigs make their own hole. Snorting and grunting, digging away, somehow they know when it's just the right size and depth. You supply the water, and they happily keep up the maintenance. Wilbur loved to put his head under the water and blow bubbles. And were they big bubbles. He would often come up with a big pile of mud on his snout.

There's nothing quite so relaxing as to see a pig fully stretched out in his very own mudhole. It must be a lot of fun to be a pig.

There's a lot to know when you're raising a pig. Hardly a day went by that I didn't discover something new.

Now, I had done much to make Wilbur comfortable, but baby oil? Yep. That's right. His skin never did smell bad, but it would get dry from the sun. In between his great big ears and the side of his head, the skin would get red from irritation. You see, that's a very soft spot of unprotected skin, and it especially needed something. A big bottle of baby oil and a big spray bottle, and you're in business.

I would spray his back, and he thought it was hog heaven. Oh, he loved it. And did he smell good.

Well, he didn't love the ear part. His ears were tender, and when you pulled them back to spray them, he protested with snorts and a shake of his head.

After a good oiling, I scratched his back. In this way pigs are like us. Now what do you scratch a pig's back with? I got the heavy garden rake and turned the teeth up and scratched his back with the smooth part. Wilbur loved this. He would wiggle with delight. Oh my, what a spoiled pig.

CHAPTER 4

Sometimes You Can't Use the Bathroom

Each day with Wilbur brought new experiences. Most were ordinary. But then something happened that brought a whole new meaning to having a pig as a pet.
Constipation!
No...him, not me. That's right, a constipated pig. You may ask, "How do you know?" Well, there was the evidence in the pen--or rather, the lack of it.

After several days I grew concerned. Wilbur had stopped eating. I knew he would need to use the bathroom if he was going to be okay.

With dread, I called the vet.

"Dr. Smith."

"What's Wilbur doing now?"

"It's what he's not doing: using the bathroom. Do you know what to do?"

"Pigs don't live long enough to get constipated, so I don't know what to do."

After several calls to different vets, one suggested I put mineral oil in Wilbur's grain. But I ignored that because he wasn't eating in the first place.

What to do? What to do? He could get sicker and die if untreated.

"Aha!" I said. The TV commercial, you know the one: the lady is not feeling well, and the announcer says to use Ex-lax and you'll feel better in the morning.

Sure enough, next morning she's standing at the opened French doors, breeze blowing through the curtains, and she's smiling like everything came out all right. Would this work on Wilbur?

I gave him three chocolate tablets and waited…and waited. All night long, and nothing.

These were desperate times that called for desperate measures. So I gave Wilbur the rest of the box. And waited.

Six hours later, I went out to his pen. There he was, standing like the lady at the French doors. Breeze blowing, curtains billowing out, Wilbur smiling, and all was well. And he'd gone in the exact same spot he always did. My, what a pig.

CHAPTER 5

Pigs May Not Be What We Think They Are

Happy days!

Pigs are stereotyped. They stink; they eat like pigs; they're always dirty; they only eat slop; they wallow in filthy mud, oblivious to the stench; they have no feelings; they do not think; they are stupid; they are lazy; they are only good for cooking and eating.

Truth is, we are wrong about all of the above. I was wrong too—that is, until I took in Wilbur as a pet. I found out that all animals were originally created to be just animals, not human food. Read it. It's in the Bible. Check out Genesis. Man only killed and ate animals after God dismissed man and woman from the Garden of Eden for misbehavior. Previously, man and woman were vegetarians.

Wilbur did not object to being clean. I washed him regularly. He did love his self-dug mudhole because that helped protect his skin. Remember, pigs do not sweat. They need the mud for protection. In most cases, pigs are kept together in confined areas and have little choice but to walk in very dirty mud. But by themselves, they will not do this. Remember reading about Wilbur's potty habits? Well, they astounded this city boy.

Wilbur showed his feelings by being with people. He loved everybody and took great joy in their visits. He would snort in different cadences as thought speaking sentences.

Wilbur was very active. Running at full speed was a particular delight. He loved to chase a ball.

"Hey, Wilbur! Get this," I would yell as I threw the ball toward the back of the yard. Scampering off, he returned the ball for the next throw.

When I lightly pinched his skin, he knew this was the signal for him to chase me, and then I would chase him. While doing this one day, a most amazing thing happened: Wilbur came up to me, lowered his head, and untied my tennis shoe with his mouth. I couldn't believe it. How did he figure this out? How did he know it was a game? How did he know I would then chase him?

Some say pigs are stupid—I don't think so. One day during the same kind of game, he came up from behind and pulled my shirttail out. Now that's a game we play as children. How did he know that would be fun? I chased him all over—he was squealing and I was laughing. I wondered what I had discovered about God's creatures that we mostly used for food.

Wilbur made friends with our Shetland sheepdog, Ashley, who had taken to being his mother when he first arrived. It must have been Ashley's herding instinct that moved her to keep Wilbur in the yard. Anytime it looked as if he might go out of bounds, Ashley ran up to him, opened her mouth, and gently closed it on Wilbur's back to hold him steady. Wilbur got the message. They grew to be great friends.

Dogs don't generally eat hog grain. But if Ashley was out when Wilbur ate, she joined him eating from the same bowl. Wilbur didn't mind.

This friendship continued for life. In another story to be told another time, David brought home a four-day-old Jersey bull that he purchased from an auction house for nineteen dollars. It was a gift for his sister. An unexpected pig, an unexpected bull—holy cow!

But the story is this: Wilbur welcomed Ashley the dog to share the same bowl without objection. But one day Norman (the little bull) moseyed up and commenced to eat with them. At this, Wilbur slung his head at Norman as if to say, "Who are you?" Norman got the message, and though they all were friends, Norman never tried to share the bowl again.

CHAPTER 6

The Factory and the UPS Man

Its employees had once manufactured Hula-Hoops and plastic doll babies. Now it made such things as stadium seats. The factory sat on several acres about two hundred feet from our house.

A big oak tree, spared when the factory was built, sat close to the side entrance, which was about one hundred feet from Wilbur's house.

Each day, the big oak enticed many factory workers to sit under its shady embrace and enjoy lunch.

Taking a midday break, I would come home and let Wilbur out of his pen, and we would play together and have fun. He loved people, and one day he ran over to greet the factory workers. That's all it took: they were eating, Wilbur was a pig, and a bond began. Now each day instead of playing, he made a beeline for the folks under the tree.

A pig enjoying lunch with people attracted others inside to come to the big open door of the factory. Wilbur saw them eating. So as soon as he'd polished off the shared goodies of the oak folks, he'd head to the open door group. Then he would come home.

One day, the UPS man pulled up for a factory delivery. Though Wilbur was stuffed and on his way home, he detoured to the stopped truck. He laid his big old head on the first step and stared at a surprised deliveryman.

"You work here?" the UPS man asked.

Wilbur answered with a snort.

"I don't know if that means yes or no," said the UPS man.

I replied, "That was his 'no' snort. He only eats here."

CHAPTER 7

Sometimes You Miss the Obvious or Pigs Can Plow

The ground around the church house was made of very hard and very red clay. The finest of shovels experienced difficulty biting into this iron-hard dirt. It was with dread that I approached any gardening or lawn chore.

Planting a small tree should have been a thing of pleasure. Yeah, sure—you'd have better luck digging in the concrete sidewalk.

Kajung! the shovel cried as it failed to make a dent in the clay. And then Wilbur showed up. He had been scampering around the yard smelling flowers and rooting in their bed.

"Go 'way, Wilbur. This is frustrating and you're getting in the way. Quit digging there!"

After thirty minutes, I had gotten nowhere. Oh well, I didn't need a tree anyhow.

I gathered the tools to park them back in the shed. I said, "Quit digging, Wilbur—whoa, wait a minute. He's turning that clay over. It can't be; the shovel wouldn't dent it, but it's sure getting out of Wilbur's way. Go for it, Wilbur! Dig all you want."

He put his head down like a backhoe, dug in, lifted up, and the big red balls of clay rolled off his huge snout.

The small tree dropped in the hole.

"Wilbur, let's go get a Little Debbie cake and wash it down with a chocolate Yoo-hoo."

Folks who drive by don't know it, but Wilbur planted all the shrubs at that house.

CHAPTER 8

Relaxing Time

What a life!

Wilbur is a giant among gentle animals. He dearly loves people. He loves you just as you are and reflects the common prayer: *Lord, help me to be the kind of person my dog thinks I am.* Except in my case, the dog would be a pig.

There always is a sense of peace about him. Stresses of the world pass him by. So just being with him brings a feeling of calm and peace. This huge, fat pig (is that a smile on his face?) is a great therapist; he just doesn't know it.

Sometimes you would find him just basking in the sun, eyes closed, seemingly oblivious to his surroundings. Yet he would snort as you walked by. Didn't matter how many times you went by, he snorted, acknowledging your presence.

The only thing Wilbur ever seemed concerned about was his bed of straw. Frequently I added new straw, and it didn't matter where he was or what he was doing—he always ran to watch. I guess he wanted to make sure I wasn't messing his bedroom up. He walked all over the fresh straw as if he were straightening the sheets on a newly made bed. When it was to his liking, he returned to whatever he had been doing.

Wilbur was always growing, and his house was always getting smaller. One day I went out to sit in his house with him and settled down on the soft straw. That's when he decided to get up and turn around.

"Wilbur, holy cow, you're squashing me up against the wall. Don't do that!"

Snort, snort, grunt, grunt, was his reply.

Then he sat down, looking me right in the face. And we talked and visited. And somehow the troubles of the day faded away.

I know it sounds nuts, but sometimes I was sure he knew what I was saying. He was not silent. He would grunt or snort his way through your conversation. It didn't matter how long I wanted to talk; he would listen.

Sometimes when I was tired and silent, Wilbur talked. No kidding—he would use different snort ranges and tones and talk away. I never knew how to answer, but I responded with something and he would continue. He was probably telling me I wasn't a good listener.

Wilbur was like this. He loved people and would talk with anyone. Somewhere in this there is a lesson for the world and us.

CHAPTER 9

The Wash Job

Cars are made to be washed; pigs aren't. Even when pigs get into water, it's a mudhole. And I mean mud. It sticks to their skin and protects them from the sun and bugs; well, most of the time it does.

I guess having dogs most of my life got me into the habit of washing my pets. I didn't see Wilbur as being any different, and because no one had told him otherwise, I hoped he'd love it.

I realized that two things could happen after his bath: he would head straight to his mudhole or the sun would burn his skin.

One, the mudhole. I couldn't do anything about that. The other I could, so I fetched the baby oil and set it aside. Next I let him out into the backyard so his whole pen wouldn't turn into a mudhole.

"Come on, Wilbur, its bath time."

He snorted with happiness while running around in circles.

"Hold still, I've got to put the shampoo on you."

I squirted him all over with no-tears shampoo, then squirted him with the hose and scrubbed him with a brush. All except the back of his ears, the tender part.

Soon he was covered in millions of bubbles, snorting his approval, followed by gallons and gallons and gallons of cool water for the rinse. He slung his head, and water droplets covered everything close by.

After his bath, I rubbed him down with baby oil. Finding that there was a lot of hide to rub, I turned to a sprayer. Wilbur liked this better. The oil felt cool and soothing. The backs of his ears, especially in the fold, always got pink and tender. When I rubbed there, he snorted deeply and pulled his head away. But when we were finished, a happier pig clearly never lived.

Our church was just across the street. For a week each year, our children gathered for vacation Bible school. During recreation time, I said, "Hey, let's go give Wilbur a bath."

I let him out of his pen, and Wilbur and twenty-five children romped and played.

"Hey, be sure he doesn't step on your foot."

They took turns squirting him with the hose. Pig squeals of delight were heard. Others took turns spraying him with baby shampoo. Others scrubbed him with a brush. Kids running, squealing, soap/water spraying, Wilbur squealing—what a show.

You could always tell when it was vacation Bible school time.

Wilbur touched a lot of lives by teaching kids that animals are special.

CHAPTER 10

Who's That Knocking?

I've never asked anyone if pigs can jump. Still haven't. And I don't know if they normally do.

But I know one that could and did.

Our back porch was at least three feet off the ground. One evening I was out in the yard and looking toward the house.

Did I see what I thought I saw? Did Wilbur just jump up on the porch? He sure did—without any effort at all.

Why?

He wanted to come inside.

How did I know?

He was hitting the door with his big nose. Margaret was in the kitchen and heard the racket and came to see.

"Wilbur, you can't come in. When you were little, it was okay...but three hundred pounds of pig in the house? I don't think so."

Despite being rejected, Wilbur continued jumping onto the porch and knocking to come in. In fact, it became a daily part of his routine.

I don't know why he didn't use the steps.

CHAPTER 11

I Smell Bacon Frying

If you've ever let your dog out to play, you know what I'm talking about. Retrieving sticks, balls, playing chase, romping, and just having fun.

Wilbur loved this and seemed to live for this time. He would romp all over the yard, snorting with delight. Folks driving by would often stop and watch.

He grew so accustomed to being out of his pen that I would leave his gate open when we worked in the yard. He would just hang with us. Wherever we went, he went.

One day it was time to cut the grass. The push mower roared to life with a big *vroom!* Up and down the yard I went, cutting smooth paths in the ragged grass. There's just something about giving your yard a haircut. The grass is so beautiful afterward.

Pushing along, I felt the presence of something beside me. It was Wilbur, happily following me up and down the yard. Trouble was, he was getting too close to the mower. I shooed him away, but he came back.

At one point I stopped to pick up a stick and throw it from the mower's path. I didn't see any reason to kill the motor, so I held on to the safety handle. Bending down, I heard above the engine's roar the sound of frying. You know, like bacon sizzling at breakfast time.

What is that? I thought.

Standing up, I saw Wilbur with his nose on the muffler. Don't ever touch a hot muffler. It will fry you. And that's exactly what it was doing to Wilbur.

Pigs must not have nerves on the sides of their nose, because Wilbur wasn't squealing. Fact is, I don't think he knew it was happening.

"You stupid pig! You're frying just like bacon. Get your nose off the muffler!"

He did.

That was the first and only time I called him stupid.

CHAPTER 12

Town without Pity

Supper time

"That pig has to go!" said the gruff voice on the phone.

"Who is this?" I responded.

"The town administrator, and you've got ten days to move that pig out of the city limits."

"What's this about? Wilbur's been here for four years. There's a factory next door, and the land owner to the rear of our house has many cows grazing on his land."

"If you don't move that pig in ten days, I'll come and move him for you."

"You say you're the town administrator? That's a strange duty for you. The town put 'pig removal' in your contract, did they?"

"You got ten days," he fumed.

Imagine my surprise as I tried to guess what was behind the demand to remove Wilbur in ten days, let alone move him at all. Wilbur had made friends far and wide. Parents would stop by so their children could visit. The factory folks next door and the UPS man loved him. Wilbur was cleaner than the town dogs that roamed freely. He didn't smell and he caused no problems.

The answer: politics, pure and simple. It seems as if someone always wants to rain on your parade. They have little joy in them and don't want others to be joyful. Some might say it's downright meanness. I think it's both.

They say you can't fight city hall. If that's true, it's especially so in a small town with small minds.

Most people couldn't believe Wilbur had been ordered to leave. Wilbur was a "people pig." Moving him back to the farm would not be good for him. Oh, he could make his way all right. And being with other pigs would help him grow in the social graces.

But it was devastating news. It was the same as someone telling you your dog must go.

The news was another of life's reminders. Some very mean people will come your way and do very mean things that you can do nothing about.

I drove over to the farm where Wilbur was born. What a sight! Fifty pigs knee-deep in stinking mud. Yuk! And not a decent place for a pig to lie down and sleep. It was dreadful to know that Wilbur would return there.

Tommy, the farm owner, was kind and agreed to let Wilbur have some space. There was a shed of sorts, full of discarded farm things and pieces of broken glass. Fixing this was going to be a chore.

Several days of work later, you could at least walk in the place. It would have to do.

To know how we all felt, imagine having your dog in the backyard where you can play with him and enjoy his companionship every day. Suddenly he's gone. Oh, you can drive four miles and visit with him, but that's little consolation. We were heartbroken.

I know in my heart that Wilbur didn't understand as we drove off and left him in his new place.

I gave the farmhand specific instructions on how to feed Wilbur. The other pigs were being fattened for market, and one thing Wilbur didn't need was more fat. Well, I might as well have hollered in the Grand Canyon for the impact my feeding request had.

The farmhand poured the feed to Wilbur. Wilbur ate and ate and ate and grew so huge his stomach herniated and dropped to the ground. He couldn't walk without stepping on his stomach. Ouch!

Meanwhile our backyard was empty without his presence. His house sat empty while the big red "WILBUR" I had painted on the side reminded us daily he was gone.

The town manager said he had to go: pigs were not allowed. He didn't say anything about wooden pigs.

Sometimes you have to make a statement, so I bought a sheet of plywood and commenced to cut out the image of a pig drawn by my wife, Margaret.

We painted it the most beautiful shade of pig pink and proudly displayed Wilbur II in our front yard.

There were no more calls from the town.

Despite our best efforts, the real Wilbur grew and grew, reaching forty-eight inches around his neck. He was huge and uncomfortable. Yet the weight didn't hurt his spirit. He was funny, playful, and loveable, just like always.

My heart hurt for him, though. I never intended for him to be so physically challenged. I had fed him carefully at home so this kind of thing wouldn't happen. Now we both would have to deal with the lifelong consequences of his overeating.

CHAPTER 13

Moving Time

I received a phone call from a church in a town about an hour away to come and interview as their potential pastor.

The church was located about five miles from the city in a slowly changing rural area. Miles of shoreline on a nearby lake were attracting new homes. Rolling pastures dotted the landscape and were sprinkled with livestock of all sorts. Wild deer, turkey, fox, and skunk freely roamed the woods and sometimes your yard, but no pigs.

Sadly, these critters would eventually have to move on as the encroaching city devoured their land.

We decided it was time to move and be pastor to these wonderful folks.

There would be room for Wilbur somewhere in this, but I decided not to tell my new congregation about Wilbur. Not yet, anyway.

My heart jumped for joy when I first saw that several acres lay behind the new church and contained only the parsonage and a distant two-car garage. My eyes envisioned a magnificent pig condominium constructed against the garage's back wall. There would be privacy and safety for Wilbur. That is, if the church folk had room in their hearts for the world's greatest pig.

We moved in, and the opportunity soon came to tell them about Wilbur. They stood with smiles as his story unfolded.

"Sure, bring him on," said the deacon.

I called Tommy right away.

"Tommy, we're coming to get Wilbur. Will you let us use your trailer?"

"Yeah, course I will."

"Okay, soon as I can build a new house and fence, I'll be over to get him."

Leland was a new friend and a member of our church. He had a farm and lots of big equipment. I called him.

"Leland, can you come and bulldoze the brush behind the garage?"

"Yeah, I reckon I can. Be there tomorrow."

"Oh, and can you dig about thirty-two post holes for the fence?"

"Yeah, I reckon I can."

I was dancing a jig at the thought of Wilbur being with us. This was going to be so much fun!

Let's see, I'll need several sheets of tin roof, big posts for the walls, plenty of fence posts, bales of straw, nails, and fencing.

"That was a lot of stuff," I said as the last post was unloaded.

I laid out an area thirty feet wide and seventy-five feet long; Leland dug the holes, and I dropped the posts and tamped the surrounding dirt to hold them strong and fast.

Now the house: ten feet wide, ten feet deep, and eight feet high. My, oh my, what a pig house.

It stood glistening in the sun. All silvery and shiny and looking so comfortable loaded with fresh straw. No landscaping was needed. Wilbur's built-in bulldozer would shape the dirt as he wanted.

I said to David, "Let's go get Wilbur."

We took the back way to Tommy's farm and bounced down the country road for an hour. It had been three months since we'd left him.

When we arrived, we found Tommy waiting on us. It was good to see Tommy: white beard, overalls, plaid shirt, and a chaw of tobacco tucked away in a face that always was happy.

"Let's load him up," Tommy said.

Pulling the truck around back, I saw Wilbur.

"Hey, Wilbur!" I shouted. He ran toward me like an eight-legged dog. I hugged him around his huge neck while he snorted and oinked with excitement.

"Wow! I can't believe how dirty you are. And you're so much bigger."

Wilbur loaded easily. Could he know that at long last we would be together again?

Thanking our friend Tommy, we pulled out for home. We could not know that it was our last time to be with Tommy. He died unexpectedly a few weeks later. We will always miss him.

David's small truck lurched down the road as the small four-cylinder engine struggled under Wilbur's weight. I kept a close eye on Wilbur and noticed he didn't sit down. He stood all the way home.

"Sit down," I kept yelling. But he stood, even when we took a shortcut back to our new home.

Have you ever taken the wrong road? Now this was the right road, but it was wrong for one reason: the rains had made it the texture of an old-timey washboard.

Chatter, chatter, our teeth seemed to cry out as we bumped and bounced all the way. And Wilbur continued to stand. I knew all this jiggling wasn't going to be good for him; that much weight on four pig feet was going to be tiring.

Finally we arrived.

David backed the truck to Wilbur's new gate, and Wilbur slowly stepped into his new pen. And that's where he stayed, just inside the gate, sleeping late into the next day.

"Welcome home, Wilbur," I said as I kissed his huge ear. "I missed you. We're going to continue our fun, and we won't have to be separated again."

CHAPTER 14

Settling In

After his long sleep, Wilbur went into his new home and set about raking the straw with his big snout. When he had it just right, he lay down like you do on a mattress for the first time.

He seemed to be saying, "Boy, this is great. It feels so soft."

He got up, leaving a perfect pig outline. In the summer, when he didn't need straw, he would lie on the dirt. Over the years the dirt sank under his tremendous size, leaving a perfect pig outline.

It's still there. Though he's gone now, I go out to the pen when I miss him. And that's often. And there he is, in that impression in the dirt and the impression in my heart.

A pig needs a mudhole. Wilbur set about digging one. His huge snout pushed deeply into the dirt and lifted up. Over and over, in and up, the dirt giving way to his powerful neck muscles.

Soon he had what would be the perfect mudhole. I filled it with water—Wilbur's own swimming pool. What more could a pig want?

There was one more thing, though. Where do you think Wilbur built the pool? That's right. In front of the gate, so you had to jump when you went in or get wet. The hole got so wide I couldn't jump it anymore, so I moved the gate. No chance of him moving the hole.

CHAPTER 15

Yoo-hoo and Moon Pies

I've been told you shouldn't give animals chocolate to eat. And with good reason—it can be deadly to some. Early on, I gave Wilbur a chocolate-covered pie with jelly in the middle. You know the kind, wrapped in cellophane and packed so many to a box. I really did this without thinking. Luckily it didn't bother him.

Feeding him sweet snacks was a fun part of his day—actually, any food was.

One day....

"Wilbur, here's your Moon Pie."

Smack, smack, smack as the treat disappeared.

"Hey, you want some chocolate milk?" I put the bottle toward his mouth—and was I surprised when he took it, held it skyward, and drank. Some went in, but most dribbled out over his fat jowls, down his neck, and splashed on the ground. From that day on he held his bottle to drink.

Wilbur loved grits. I didn't give them to him much, though. They would get stuck between his gums and jowls and he would spend the day trying to get them out. If he'd only had fingers.

Same for peanut butter. Except it stuck to the roof of his mouth. His tongue would tire out trying to loosen the butter. If he'd only had fingers.

CHAPTER 16

And You Thought You Didn't like Going to the Dentist?

There are two things that will grow too long if a hog lives long enough: teeth and hooves. Add this to the list of hog facts I did not know.

Sure enough, Wilbur's teeth grew too long. A tusk emerged from each side of his mouth—great big tusks that were growing back toward his face. I knew he would be in trouble if something wasn't done. Yes, I had better sense than to look under "Dentist" in the phone book. It should have come as no surprise that if no one treats constipation in a pig, then there are no pig dentists.

There's a school for veterinarians in Georgia, and I called them.

"Doctor, I need to cut Wilbur's tusks and don't know how without hurting him."

"Don't worry, the tusks have no feeling, no nerves. They are like very hard chalk. You can use almost anything to cut them."

You probably know by now that this was not going to be easy.

What to use as a cutting tool? Hacksaw? No, Wilbur wouldn't hold still for this and I might cut him. Bolt cutters? They're big and heavy, able to cut through steel. Yeah, that might do it.

I bought what looked like the right size. Which taught me another thing: bolt cutters have long handles but don't open very wide. So I bought the largest ones Walmart had and prepared for Pig Dentistry 101.

Wilbur was asleep under a shade tree in his pen. I figured I would get one chance at best to see if my scheme would work. Quietly, slowly, I snuck up on him. Now this was awkward, sneaking and opening the long handles of the bolt cutters that required my arms to be spread out wide. Would they go around his tusks? What if I missed?

Wilbur snorted but didn't open his eyes. The cutter slipped around the tusk, and I pulled the handles closed as hard as I could. *POW!*

I keep learning with this pig. Tusks sound like firecrackers when cut with bolt cutters. *Bang!*

The tusk flew through the air. I jumped back. Wilbur jumped up, snorting to the high heavens (somehow I knew he wasn't going to let me at the other tooth).

The tusk cut cleanly, but the sound scared Wilbur. I got the other one later when he was sleeping.

From that day on, Wilbur looked for bolt cutters when I entered his pen. Even when I tried to hide them, he seemed to have radar and would pick up on them, and off he would run.

He got better at running, and I got worse at hiding the cutters. One day the tusks had grown so long they began to cut into his face. They had to be cut. Somehow I needed to figure out a way to hold Wilbur still. Maybe Jerry had a device that would work.

Jerry was another friend who owned a farm and might know what to do. I called him.

"Hello, Jerry? I don't have a hog gate to hold Wilbur. Any ideas?"

"Yeah, we can tie a rope around his head, attach it to my bumper, and I'll back up slowly until the tension holds his head."

"Wow! I don't know about this."

"It won't hurt, and it's the only way. I'll be over in a little while."

"Okay."

Jerry came, and I coaxed Wilbur over to the fence. I tied the rope around his head with Wilbur looking at me as if to say, "What in the world are you doing?"

I passed it through the fence, and Jerry tied it to the bumper. The truck roared to life and started backward and Wilbur started squealing. Well, squealing might not do justice to the loudest pig wailing ever heard in Greenwood County.

I was nervous and shaking all over. He was scared, and it shook me. With shaking hands I did the worst job of pig tooth cutting in history. Jerry was shook too, except he was shaking with laughter at the sight.

Wilbur was mad for three days and had little to do with me. He obviously didn't think I was a good dentist. That's okay. I didn't think he was a good patient.

CHAPTER 17

A Pig Girdle?

My stomach is so big!

Wilbur had a stomach hernia, a big one, a *really* big one. He had grown so large that his stomach muscles couldn't hold the weight, and they just let go.

The hernia started small, and I didn't worry too much about it. Remember, this was my first and only pig, and I didn't know their soft underbellies could give way. Pigs don't usually live long enough for this to happen—ever seen one with a hernia?

Soon his dropped to the ground and dragged along as he walked. It got worse. Now it was really dragging. He stepped on parts of it with his back hooves when he walked.

The skin would bruise and sometimes there was blood. He was a sad sight. Wilbur didn't let this stop him. He went where he wanted, just took his time trying not to step on himself.

It was time to call Dr. Stuart for advice.

"Hello, Dr. Stuart. Wilbur has a stomach hernia, and I wanted to know if surgery might help him."

"Well, it would, but he's too big. I mean, I don't think he would survive the anesthesia. He will have to live with it."

That was something I didn't want to hear. Wilbur had survived so much: starvation, pneumonia, constipation, overfeeding, and several moves. Surely after all this there must be a way to lift his stomach up. But what?

Margaret said, "I've got an idea, but you will think it's crazy."

"Tell me, please," I replied. "It can't be any crazier than some of the things we've done for Wilbur."

I wasn't prepared. Believe me, I wasn't. I bet you didn't think of it either.

"A girdle," she replied.

"What! We'll be the laughingstock of the county. A pig girdle...I can hear the laughter already."

"If we can make it work, it will help so much."

"I know, I know. I just can't imagine."

Little did we know (again) what we were getting into as we drove into the Walmart parking lot to buy the materials for a pig girdle.

I can promise you that in the history of man, no one has gone into Walmart to buy cloth to make a girdle for a pig. No one at any time in any city in any place in the world has bought cloth to make a pig girdle from Walmart.

We didn't know what we were doing, so Margaret volunteered to figure it out. She chose a netted material. If you've seen a shrimp net, you know what I mean.

Good idea, I thought.

"That way water can drain."

We bought bunches of cloth and several yards of Velcro and headed home.

Something we didn't think about: It was easy to measure around Wilbur's middle, but what about the part lying on the ground? Margaret and I tried and tried to pick that part up, but it was too heavy. This is where the alarm should have sounded. If you can't lift that heavy stomach up, how are you going to put a girdle on him? But we plodded merrily on, not realizing.

We measured and measured, Margaret sewed and sewed, and finally the girdle was made. I can only describe it by saying that it looked more like a shrimp net than anything else.

It was hot outside.

"Margaret, go 'round the other side, and I'll slide the girdle under Wilbur's stomach to you." His stomach was pink, soft, and wrinkled and seemed to weigh a ton. I could lift only small pieces as I slid the material toward Margaret.

"Why am I sweating so much and he looks so cool?"

"Okay, pull it toward you."

"I've got it."

"Okay, let's stand and lift at the same time."

"Okay, lift."

Yeah, right.

"Lift, lift!" I yelled.

Pigs don't sweat, but humans do. I was soaked. I looked over Wilbur's back and saw a soaked, exhausted Margaret.

"I don't think this is working," she said. "Besides, the girdle's too small."

"You're kidding. You mean…?"

"Yep, back to the sewing machine."

Well, not exactly. We thought we had hit on a solution for his problem, but sometimes an invention just doesn't work. And we decided this was one.

A pig girdle. We still have the world's one and only. Don't look for it on eBay.

CHAPTER 18

Running Water and the Pig Fountain

A pig drinks a lot of water every day—seems like a bathtub full. Wilbur's new home was behind the church garage some distance from the house. Hauling buckets of water soon became a real chore. What to do? I hated to admit it, but installing running water was the only solution.

Can you believe that? One pig, and he has to have running water! The house had at one time been on a plumbing system from the church well. Though no longer in use, it still was capable of delivering water.

The distance was over one hundred feet, making it impractical to dig a trench by hand. So I borrowed a ditchdigger from a friend and dug a ditch back to Wilbur's pen. At the local hardware store, I bought pipe, a pipe cutter, glue, various spigots, and odds and ends. (This pig was costing some money!)

After two hard days of work on my part, Wilbur became the only pig in the county (maybe state) to have his own personal spigot with endless water. He loved it. And was it convenient.

For a while all went well. Then I learned my next pig lesson: *never* put a water spigot where a pig can get to it.

Church service begins at seven on Wednesday night and I walked out to Wilbur's pen to check on him.

Oh no! Is that what I think it is? Water squirting like a huge fountain straight up in the air! And Wilbur playing like he was at Water World. Running in and out and around, splashing, squealing, and having a ball.

He had bitten the spigot off. I dashed to find a cutoff valve and stopped the water. Moral: Always install the spigot outside the fence.

CHAPTER 19

Calling All Cars

Scratching Wilbur's back

The police radio crackled to life.

"Be on the lookout for Wilbur the pig. Description as follows: about seven feet long, thirty-five to forty inches tall, weighs approximately nine hundred pounds, no tail. Last seen in vicinity of Willard Road. Pig is friendly."

In the annals of police history, no APB had ever been issued for a pig. Here's how it happened.

Wilbur's pen was really big. Lots of roaming room accompanied his large tin home. He had dug a mudhole that was just the right size. It stayed full of water. I put in bleach weekly to keep it clean. When it rained, I fed him inside his house so his grain wouldn't get wet. In the winter, stacks of fluffy hay kept him warm. When his water froze, warm water was carried to him. In summer, he was rubbed down with baby oil so his skin didn't dry out. I scratched his back with the flat side of a garden rake. Yoo-hoo chocolate drink, Little Debbie cakes, and assorted goodies were his.

What more could a pig want?

His pen was as secure as I could make it; the idea was to keep animals out rather than Wilbur in. Silly me. I didn't think about the gate. He simply put his big snout under it and lifted up. Off the hinges it came, and freedom was his.

Why the urge to roam? Maybe it was the freedom he had enjoyed in the early days. Who knows? But roam he did. Now he was huge and had difficulty walking. Remember that his stomach dragged the ground and that he would step on it with his back hooves. How far could he have gone?

Where was he? What direction? What if Wilbur got on the road? I was scared and worried for his safety, but also for others'. Running into nine hundred pounds of pig would be like hitting concrete. I didn't want someone hurt. What to do?

I ran in and called the sheriff.

"Sheriff's office. What's your emergency?"

"Ma'am, my pig has escaped!"

"Your what has done what?"

"My pig has escaped. His name is Wilbur, he's huge, and if a car hits him, it will hurt someone. I need you to let the police know so they can be on the lookout."

"What's he look like?"

"A pig, a really big one. I gave her Wilbur's description.

"All right, sir, I'll let the sheriff know."

I hung up, and now I was at a dead run looking all over, and I couldn't find him. Fifteen minutes then twenty minutes passed and no Wilbur. My fright turned to panic. When did he get out? He moved so slowly, where could he be?

Then I noticed a break in the back woods just wide enough that a pig might get through. On the other side, a hundred yards or so, lay a dead-end road with six homes.

It seemed impossible he could walk that far. But since it was the only place I'd not searched, I took off.

The trees flew by as I ran. Out of breath as I cleared the woods, I stood for a moment scanning the rural dead-end street.

There he was, stepping onto a man's driveway on which stood the biggest, meanest-looking dog I'd ever seen.

CHAPTER 20

Cheez Doodles and the Big Mean Dog

The big mean dog was the picture of the perfect watchdog. He was in the driveway restrained by a logging chain. Now I'm not talking about your average chain. It was made of big links; nothing you have in your garage would cut it, not even the bolt cutters we used to trim Wilbur's tusks. The owner must have thought he was a brute; no one was going to argue that point. The unwritten message was: "Don't come in my yard."

As I got closer, I noticed a change had come over this watchdog. He looked shocked and very meek. Here I was, a stranger, and he ignored me. He was not behaving as if he were protecting his master's property; in fact, he looked puzzled. There, standing next to the watchdog, was a very large creature and a big pile of Cheez Doodles.

I had found Wilbur.

Wilbur was munching away on the dog's snack. There was no sign of fear of the dog in him. Wilbur had grown up in safety and saw no danger in the watchdog. Lucky for Wilbur, I guess, or maybe it was the dog that was lucky.

Dogs would often pass Wilbur's pen on the way to somewhere else. They would stroll by the garage completely unaware and unprepared for the huge animal just around the corner. They would leave quickly.

CHAPTER 21

Get in the Trailer, Wilbur!

The long walk had exhausted Wilbur, and I knew it was too far for him to walk back. The sun was disappearing into the trees, and darkness was coming. I tested him to see if he would follow me.

"Wilbur, quit eating the dog's Cheez Doodles and let's go home!"

Snort was his reply.

"Wilbur, let's go!"

Snort, snort.

He didn't want to go. So what did he do? He turned around and headed next door and sat down in the lady's front yard. Wilbur could be stubborn and hardheaded. This time he was both.

The young girl standing inside her screen door hollered, "Mama, Mama, come quick! You won't believe what's in our front yard."

"Ma'am, I'm sorry Wilbur's sat down in your yard."

"That's all right, he looks like he sure could use some water. Get the bucket, honey, and get that hog something to drink."

By this time, all the neighbors had come to look. They gathered close to see this strange sight.

Wilbur slurped and slurped the cool water. It ran down his jowls, dripping on the ground. Pleased and refreshed, he threw his head up and around and let out the biggest, loudest snort you ever heard. The neighbors scattered in fright.

"No, no, it's okay. He won't hurt you. That's just his way."

Slowly they regrouped, just not as close.

I'd never seen a pig root while sitting down. I especially didn't want to now. Pigs have very strong neck muscles capable of breaking the toughest soil using their nose and head like an old-timey steam shovel.

Wouldn't you know it? Wilbur began to dig into the manicured lawn, taking out big scoops each time.

"Stop it!" I hollered. "Ma'am, I'm sorry he's messing up your yard. I'll come back tomorrow and repair it. I promise."

"That's all right. Reckon you can't stop him. Don't look like nobody could."

"Stop it, Wilbur!"

That's when I noticed a car pulling up. It was the highway patrol. An officer with a clean, freshly pressed uniform got out.

"I heard the APB to be on the lookout for this giant pig. Never heard anything on the radio like that. Thought I might cruise around and see if I could spot him. I just had to see for myself. Boy, he's big."

"Yes sir, and he's friendly too. Trouble is, he won't get up."

Suddenly Wilbur stood; the crowd ran. Sort of reminded me of the undersea pictures I've seen. You know, where there's a big school of fish all swimming along together and one changes direction and then they all do.

"I told you he's friendly."

Packed together like schooled fish, they slowly returned.

"How am I going to get you home?" I said to Wilbur. "Here you are, a pig in cow country. You sure got us in a situation. It's getting darker, and you can't stay out here all night."

Then it hit me.

I couldn't leave him. Now wasn't that something? The possibility of spending the night with a huge pig in a stranger's front yard. All young boys must grow up with that dream. The night dew will lay its cover, my bones will ache, and I'll wake sore and wet. I can't wait. At least I can use his soft, flabby, fat stomach as a pillow.

Surely there must be someone who can help get us home tonight...Jerry! He keeps cows! He has a trailer!

"Hello, Jerry, Wilbur's escaped from his pen. It's getting dark, and I've got to get him home. Can you bring your trailer and help? We're behind the church on Simms Road."

Laughter, lots of it. "I'll be there as soon as I can."

What a relief to see him backing the trailer up to Wilbur. We'd be home shortly, or so I thought. What we didn't know was that Wilbur had turned in for the night and wasn't going anywhere.

Pigs don't come with instructions. There's nothing written to tell you how to move a stubborn nine-hundred-pound pig. To make matters worse, the trailer was not ground level. And this pig was too tired to step up.

My patience grew thin after thirty minutes of "*Get up and get in the trailer!*" That's when I saw the piece of lumber; it was a two-by-four about four feet long. No, I didn't hit him with it, at least not yet.

I wedged the two-by-four under his behind and lifted with all my strength. Wilbur just grunted. I nearly collapsed. This time Jerry and I both lifted. Same results, no movements, just another Wilbur grunt.

It's surprising how much you can sweat after the sun goes down. Many tries later, I was soaked. I was running out of options.

Wilbur, all you have to do is stand up, get in the trailer, and we can go home. It's simple. Why are you being this way?

Pushing didn't work; maybe pulling would. Jerry had a rope, and I put it around Wilbur's neck. We pulled and pulled and pulled and pulled. All we had for our efforts so far were aching muscles, drenched clothes, and a bored pig.

Now God knows I've never hit a pig before, especially this one. But I'd had it; no more Mr. Nice Guy. Where's that two-by-four?

Smack! The stick landed right across his big butt. The crowd jumped, the highway patrol left, and Wilbur grunted. Otherwise nothing changed.

So I resorted to lifting and smacking. Finally, after two incredible hours, Wilbur stood up, put one foot in the trailer, and walked in.

The crowd shouted with joy. Jerry was relieved that he could finally return home, and we rattled down the rocky, bumpy road singing wee, wee, wee all the way.

CHAPTER 22

We Don't Have a Record for Oldest Pig

I was proud of Wilbur. I wanted the world to know of him. But how do you do that? There are no "greatest pig" contests. The news media wouldn't be interested. Or would they?

The *Guinness Book of World Records*, I thought. Maybe they had pig categories. What would Wilbur qualify for? Maybe world's fattest hog, or world's oldest hog.

I asked Wilbur, and he thought fattest wouldn't be the way he wanted to be remembered. So I sent in the information about his age and waited and waited and waited for a response.

One day the response came in the mail. We jumped up and down just knowing our Wilbur had made it into the book. I tore the envelope open.

"We are sorry. We do not have a category for the world's oldest pig."

Talk about disappointment. I told Wilbur. Boy, was he mad.

"Boss"—that's what he called me—"they don't have a category? Everything's got to start somewhere. They didn't have a lot of categories until somebody did something. Why can't they start one for me?"

"Beats me, Wilbur. I thought that's what they were all about."

"Do you think it's because I'm a pig?"

"I don't know, but I think *Guinness* is missing out by not including you."

We never found out if Wilbur was the oldest pig or if there was an older one. So I started my own record book. Wilbur lived to be almost eleven. Do you know one older?

CHAPTER 23

Angels in the Pigpen

There is a prayer, and it goes this way: *Lord, let me be the kind of person my dog thinks I am.* I certainly go along with this. With what I know about Wilbur, I would change it to, *Lord, let me be the kind of person my pig thinks I am.*

That's the relationship we had. A pig that loved all saw something special in me.

Wilbur provided many days of fun, laughter, and fellowship. He was a comfort. On some of my most exhausting and frustrating days, Wilbur sat with great patience and listened as I told him of my troubles.

Life has its own way of bringing joy. And when joy comes, you wish it to last forever. And it can, both in the wonder of the moment and in the time bank of memories. The sadness of now, the joy of memories.

I'll remember that day forever. It would happen on a Saturday....

Wilbur's appetite slowed along with his daily routine. I knew he didn't feel well but hoped it would pass. He'd been the picture of health, so it worried us all when he quit eating altogether. It was in the back of my mind, however, that he was ten years old.

Dr. Stuart, the retired vet in our church, came to check Wilbur.

"Can't seem to find anything wrong. Could be the heat, but with pigs it's hard to tell."

Over the next few days we kept him as comfortable as we could. I stayed with him as much as I could, laying wet towels across his big body to cool him.

Saturday came, and nothing had changed. But after lunch, everything did. Wilbur had a seizure, then another and another. Dr. Stuart came and said he didn't think it would be long before Wilbur died.

We were crushed. Tears flowed freely. Wilbur lay in the middle of his pen. My wife, Margaret, sat down and laid his head in her lap. David and I got as close as we could. Wilbur looked us in the eye. If we moved slightly, his eyes would follow. The oinks were gone. No more squeals of delight. He was too weak.

Yet this pig or hog—this animal that the world sees mostly as food—communicated to us through his eyes. He seemed to know the time was close. I swear, as I watched his eyes, I got the feeling he was reviewing his life with us. And I saw a look of approval.

It was as if he were saying, "Thank you. You have been my friends."

I was distraught. We all were. Margaret talked to him continuously to try to let him know we were there for him. We all realized the end was near and he was not going to live. Wilbur was obviously in pain. His breathing was labored as he struggled to stay with us. He did not want to die.

As hard as it was to do, Margaret decided we had to tell him it was all right to go, we would be right there with him, and we would see him again someday. He almost seemed to be waiting on this to be said.

Margaret leaned over and whispered to Wilbur how much we dearly loved him and that it was okay to let go.

The sun was setting, casting a glow about Wilbur's pen. I felt the presence of God's angels. Think about that. I did. As a minister, I had experienced this feeling before. But this was a first.

God's angels in a pigpen—could that be? Could God care that much about a pig? The presence of peace seemed all around. Something special was happening: something very special.

Yes, God cares that much. Wilbur took a long last look at us and gently closed his eyes. This great big, beautiful, wonderful pig and special friend was dead.

It seemed forever before we could move. Ever so gently and lovingly, Margaret laid Wilbur's head on a folded towel. We came together and cried buckets of tears.

Wilbur's buried there, by his pen. If you visit, you'll find a large container of flowers and a plaque that reads:
Wilbur
One Terrific Pig

CHAPTER 24

Will Animals Be in Heaven?

Many people wonder whether animals will be in Heaven. If you believe in God and His heaven, you know His people go there, but animals? I'm often asked my opinion and am always glad to give it.

I believe animals have a place in God's heaven. Why would we exclude them? Because they are lesser than we humans? If that's your view, I invite you to consider the following:

Why would God save them for the ark and abandon them in heaven? If they were significant in His sight that He would go to the enormous trouble to round them up, build a ship big enough to hold them, why would He then let them disappear from all His creation? It just doesn't make sense to think they evaporate into nothing, never to be seen or enjoyed again.

We must especially consider Revelation 19:11–16, where Jesus and the white horses are described:

> 11 Now I saw heaven opened, and behold, a white horse. And He who sat on him was called Faithful and True, and in righteousness He judges and makes war. 12 His eyes were like a flame of fire, and on His head were many crowns. He had a name written that no one knew except Himself. 13 He was clothed with a robe dipped in blood, and His name is called The Word of God. 14 And the armies in heaven, clothed in fine linen, white and clean, followed Him on white horses. 15 Now out of His mouth goes a sharp sword, that with it He should strike the nations. And He Himself will rule them with a rod of iron. He Himself treads the winepress of the fierceness and

wrath of Almighty God. 16 And He has on His robe and on His thigh a name written: King Of Kings And Lord Of Lords.

Now where will these animals come from? Will Jesus snap His fingers and the horses appear from nothing, all bridled, saddled, and ready to go? While He's certainly capable of this miracle, it seems an unlikely solution. I would think they are already there and that animals are honored in God's heaven.

I know Wilbur's there. One day he and I will walk the golden streets together. Look for us; you can't miss us—Wilbur's butt portion of ham is so big it looks like the moon over Miami, and I'll be the short guy.

Yes, there were angels in the pigpen that day.

Epilogue

Someday, your young person will show up with a stray animal and say, "Dad, can we keep him?" And you'll think about all the trouble this creature will be and how long the promise "Please, Dad, I'll clean up and feed him" will last, and you'll say, "NO!"

Take it from someone who's been there: you just might learn a lot about life and yourself if you say yes.

Thank you, David, for bringing Wilbur to us. Thank you, Leslie, for loving Wilbur so much. Thank you, Margaret, for being you.

Made in the USA
Coppell, TX
11 October 2023